THE CAR CRASH MANUAL

After the Crash - Navigating the Maze of Doctors, Lawyers , and Insurance Companies

Avi Gopin, MA, LPC

FINDING THE HELP YOU NEED.

NAVIGATING THE MAZE OF DOCTORS, LAWYERS, AND INSURANCE COMPANIES AFTER AN AUTOMOBILE ACCIDENT

- LAWYERS   - What makes a good lawyer ?
- DOCTORS   - Finding the right doctors for your injuries.
- INSURANCE - How to navigate through auto insurance procedures and policies.

1. Are you are in moderate to constant pain days or weeks after the accident ?

2. Don't feel like yourself ?

3. Have you hit your head or your head just does not feel right ?

4. Are you anxious about driving and not driving like you used to ?

5. Are you not sleeping well at night and/or feel tired/fatigued during the day ?

6. Do you feel sad, or depressed and can't figure out why ?

7. Do you feel isolated from family and friends - like they don't understand you or what you are going through ?

HEALING FROM A CAR CRASH IS A FULL TIME JOB :

A. Going to many doctors and therapy appointments per week.

B. Calls to and from your insurance company.

C. Bills, bills, and more bills - Paperwork to sift through daily.

D. Appointments with lawyers, court dates, and meetings with judges.

ALL THIS WHILE YOU'RE IN PAIN AND NOT FEELING WELL.

I am writing this book to help people navigate the complicated world of lawyers, doctors, and insurance companies following a moderate to severe accident.

I cannot tell you how many people I have witnessed suffer degradation, and further loss of house, spouse, and sense of self, due to this process.

The very process that is designed to help you can sometimes damage you even more.

I've seen people become suicidal, severely depressed, addicted to medications or self medicating because their doctors would not prescribe pain medications after a certain point.

Every delay in treatment, every botched IME, every non payment and non authorization of services prolongs the agony of the suffering individual.

In my twenty years of practice as a psychotherapist, I have seen and heard lots of horror stories.

I have seen people come into my office after a bad car accident and exclaim that they are no longer the person they used to be. Before the accident they were hard working, mentally and physically healthy and active with good family and social lives.

After the accident, all these areas of their lives have been changed. They do not sleep well, are afraid to drive, some cannot work due to their injuries, and they may be depressed or anxious - not socializing, wanting to stay at home alone without knowing why, etc.

I also see some people who, before the accident, had a precarious life fraught with some depression, anxiety, and maybe some physical ailment.

Then the accident happens and all these previous conditions are magnified. Not to mention that their whole world has been turned upside down.

The ability to make a living, to contribute to society, to socialize with friends, to have to depend on others to drive you places because you are too afraid to drive or afraid to go out of the house all are affected by the accident.

The fear of another accident, the fear of your children or those you love getting into an accident - and curtailing their life because of your fears is very prevalent.

I also see families getting into more fights with spouses and children because of fear and frustration.

These are the real day to day costs of the accident.

Some insurance companies, some doctors, and some lawyers do not understand or care about these hidden costs.

IN FACT, I CAN TELL YOU THAT IF YOU HAVE NOT BEEN IN A SERIOUS ACCIDENT YOURSELF, THEN YOU CANNOT POSSIBLY UNDERSTAND WHAT THE ACCIDENT VICTIM IS GOING THROUGH - PHYSICALLY, MENTALLY, OR EMOTIONALLY.

Most accident victims walk and talk normally for the most part and just looking at them you may think nothing is wrong.

In the beginning, they may wear a cast or splint, but eventually that comes off and the pain and the internal turmoil are essentially invisible to most people.

Some accident victims like to pretend that nothing happened - they may be in denial of the accident's severity. They courageously go back to work only to make mistakes at work, or are afraid to drive to and from work, or are not sleeping at night and are fatigued midday or all day.

Other people just don't feel like themselves and just can't seem to get back on track. And some people totally fall apart after an accident, feeling that that their whole world has fallen apart and can't be put back together again.

Maybe this seems a little melodramatic, but it happens to many, at least temporarily, until they become familiar with the new terrain. Change is more difficult for some people than for others.

For those suffering out there - YOU ARE NOT ALONE

THERE IS HELP AND GUIDANCE TOWARD GETTING BETTER.

This book is also intended for those in power of making important medical and financial decisions over people's lives- not to just look at the bottom line, and start including the human dimension more often.

After the accident, it seems to be all paperwork and business.

Not all companies are guilty of these abuses, but it does happen more than one would like.

In the final analysis:

DO YOUR RESEARCH

ADVOCATE FOR YOURSELF

WATCH WHAT YOU SIGN

TAKE CARE OF YOURSELF

BRING YOURSELF AND YOUR FAMILY TO COUNSELING - IT HELPS

CHAPTER ONE - LAWYERS

THE 1ST STEP - FIND A GOOD LAWYER
IT IS NOT AS EASY AS YOU THINK.

WHAT TO LOOK FOR :

1. Make sure he/she specializes in personal injury - that means that at least 90% of his/her practice is devoted to fighting for the rights of injured parties.

2. Make sure your lawyer is certified by his/her own State Supreme Court as a Civil Trial Attorney - you would be surprised at how few Certified Civil Trial Attorneys there are.

3. Whatever you do, do not choose a friend of the family who is a lawyer - Personal injury is complicated and requires a specialist in the field. Ask some people you trust to recommend a good lawyer, also ask your treating doctors.

4. Make sure he/she has had years of experience and a good track record. Has he handled successfully to conclusion at least an excess of 100 personal injury cases ? Don't be embarrassed to ask.

5. Can he provide you with articles on cases he has handled that have been published in law journals, etc. ?

6. Does he have printed references from clients who he has successfully handled personal injury cases for? Google the law firm and the lawyer - check out their stats.

7. Is your lawyer a member of the AAJ (American Association for Justice) and their state ATLA (Association of Trial Lawyers America) ?

8. Can your attorney provide you with actual video recordings of his or her opening remarks or summation during a personal injury trial ?

9. In personal injury cases, most lawyers work on contingency basis. This means they get about 1/3 of your settlement or judgment money if you win, and nothing if you lose. The quality of your medical treatment should not suffer whether you win or lose your case. Your lawyer should be just as competent and responsive to your needs whether or not he has what he /she considers to be a winning case or not.

A GOOD LAWYER:

a. Answers your calls or gets back to you within 24-48 hours of your call excluding holidays and weekends.

b. Advocates for you with insurance companies, hospitals, and doctors.

c. Writes letters for you to insurance companies, work, school, and occasionally to doctors when needed.

d. Calls insurance agents, case managers, or adjusters when needed to make sure you are getting the services you need.

e. If services are denied, he helps you through the appeals process to get back on track with your therapies.

f. Files motions in court if needed to get what you need.

g. Takes the time to explain your case to you - the whole process from start to finish.

h. Explains the LEGAL LINGO to you in easy to understand language:
    1. Arbitration
    2. Interrogatories
    3. Depositions
    4. Settlement
    5. Jury Award Determination
    6. PIP suit

   i. Explains the INSURANCE LINGO so you can understand it:

      1. IME - Independent Medical Evaluations

      2. The Pre-certification Process

      3. Co payment penalties

      4. Essential Services

      5. Medical Review

      6. Appeals process

      7. Law suit threshold

   j. Suggests doctors or treatments that you might need and/or points you in the right direction.

   k. Documents your injuries with pictures of bruises, bleeding, surgeries, and procedures.

   l. Suggests you have a pain journal, and a doctor and insurance journal that documents your daily pain levels and all your conversations with doctors and insurance companies - fax whenever possible - send mail return receipt requested.

Have your proof ready because insurance companies sometimes lose or misplace records and files.

WHEN SHOULD I CHANGE LAWYERS IF I AM NOT SATISFIED:

1. Doesn't return my phone calls in a timely fashion.

2. Is not going to bat for me when I have problems with my insurance company, doctors, job, or school.

3. Is not telling me what to expect in the future.

4. Is not providing me with direction to how to get the services or treatments that I need to get better.

5. Is not writing letters or filing motions in court when my insurance company denies treatments.

6. Does not have the proper credentials and refuses to share with me his statistics regarding caseload and affiliations mentioned above.

Typical questions :

1. Can I change lawyers if I am not satisfied with mine ?

   Yes - but the sooner the better, as the lawyers will have to work out the split of the settlement at the end.

2. My lawyer tells me that my case is not worth much . What does this mean, and what can I do about it ?

   A case's worth is dependent on several variables :

   a) Your insurance coverage and especially the other person's insurance coverage. You can only collect their policy limit in most cases.

   b) No Law suit threshold - This is an option that costs more in premiums but is definitely worth it in an accident. If you have the ability to sue, this entitles you to try to recoup your losses for pain and suffering, lost wages, loss of quality of life, etc. In a basic policy, you may elect the lawsuit threshold option - This means there is a limit on your ability to sue another person. No threshold means no limit . ALWAYS SELECT NO LAW SUIT THRESHOLD. It may mean more money short term but if you are hurting from an accident and it has totally changed your family, work, and social life - you are entitled to compensation in addition to healing medical injuries.

   c) Was the driver who hit me insured, underinsured ?

   If not, you may have to go after your own insurance policy for uninsured or underinsured drivers. This will depend on your coverage for these events.

   d) Am I underinsured?

   If both you and the person who hit you do not have adequate collision and liability coverage, then there is only that amount to draw from in a settlement.

   e) The physical findings also called objective evidence -

These are medical tests that prove that you sustained a serious injury in the accident. Nerve damage, seizures, muscle and ligament tears, herniated discs, displacement, and fractures. The more physical proof of injury, the more the case is worth.

3. The person who hit me had little/no insurance, can I still receive good treatment ?

Yes.

You still have to get your medical expenses paid and your insurance foots the bill.

A good lawyer will work just as hard on this kind of case, because he knows that you may be a potential future client or a referral source for other patients.

You also can check your policy for underinsured or uninsured drivers and collect from that part of your own insurance policy.

4. My lawyer gets a third of my earnings in a settlement or judgment. Are there more hidden legal expenses that I should know about ? Yes.

a) office expenses such as phone calls on your behalf

b) copies of medical or insurance or legal documents

c) motions filed in court may cost hundreds of dollars

d) expert witnesses for your trial, if you end up going to trial, (90% of cases do not go to trial) may cost thousands of dollars

5. What do I do if I think the accident was my fault ?

You are not in any position to judge fault at the scene of the accident.

Whatever you do , DO NOT ADMIT FAULT OR SAY YOU ARE SORRY TO THE OTHER DRIVER.

This may be used against you later. Even the police report may be inaccurate.

Let your lawyer help you decide your percentage of fault, if any.

<u>Comparative negligence</u> is the legal term that determines percentage of carelessness of both parties in an accident.

This will ultimately have an effect on the resulting damages to be paid.

In most states, you can't recover anything if you were more than 50% responsible for the accident.

    6. How do I know if I should go see a lawyer after my accident ?

        a) Even if you were a passenger or it wasn't your car or you were a pedestrian - if you are hurting and have to see doctors then you should also consult an attorney.

        b) If a death occurred as a result of your accident go see an attorney.

        c) If the Police report does not describe the accident accurately to your version of what happened

        d) If who caused the accident is not clear then go seek counsel

        e) If your insurance company is not supporting you and thinks you may be at fault, then go see an attorney.

Finally, in addition to all the information above, do not forget to trust your gut feelings. If you feel that your lawyer is confident, will go to bat for you, is not afraid to answer any of your questions, and looks you square in the eye, then look at their credentials and look at their character- then make up your mind. If you feel like the lawyer is talking down to you or dismisses your questions as unimportant think twice before signing on the dotted line.

THE SETTLEMENT PHASE

The settlement phase begins with your record of the events on the day of your accident. Your accounts of what happened - your injuries sustained past and present, your daily pain/anxiety diary, and your doctor's notes.

After you have finished treating with your doctors, whether or not you have healed you begin the settlement phase.

In the settlement phase, your lawyer and the insurance company lawyers are trying to determine how much money it will take to settle the claim.

If all parties agree, money is awarded. If not, the case goes to court for a jury trial.

80-90% of the cases are settled out of court.

Settlement phases can last a short or long time - months to years. More likely it will last for years.

Every case is different and the people in an accident are very different and have different needs and wants. Some just want money to pay bills . Others do not want anything except to get better. Some want to settle just to get it over with. Others feel justified in getting just compensation for their losses.

Don't rush through this phase- think it through .

Handle your settlement with your lawyer - don't try to go it alone.

Settlement awards are based on several factors -

1. You as a person - what a jury would think of you - are you believable, etc. . Many factors go into this assessment.
2. Your actual property damage - the car wreck

3. Your medical costs

4. Length of time for your healing and the severe nature of your injuries

5. Objective evidence tests, X-rays, MRIs etc.

6. Past and present health care expeneses.

7. Past and future pain and suffering.

INTERROGATORIES, DEPOSITIONS, AND ARBITRATION

INTERROGATORIES :

They are reams of paper sent to you by the other person's insurance for you and your lawyer to fill out as to your account of the accident. The statements that you use here will be tried to be used against you in the deposition phase so be careful to answer simply, truthfully, and to the point.

Don't embellish too much.

DEPOSITION :

The insurance companies involved in the accident depose you and the other driver to get your out of court recounting of the accident.

It's like a court case but without a judge and jury. The facts are recounted, recorded and compared against your earlier statements.

This will alert the other insurance company as to whether you will make a good witness or not.

First, your lawyer asks you to recount the accident and your injuries and how it has affected your life. Your lawyer asks you straight forward questions so you can get a chance to tell your side of the story without interruptions.

Then the other lawyer asks similar questions. Their questions are sometimes tricky. He wants you to have doubts about what happened and your level of responsibility.

Make no mistake- how you present yourself and how you speak is important here. They are sizing you up as a witness and will decide settlement costs partly based on this.

Deposition can take from an hour to two hours.

Just answer his questions clearly and truthfully and do not volunteer information that is not asked of you.

If you don't remember, just say I don't remember. Your lawyer will also coach you before depositions begin.

ARBITRATION:

If you are unable to come to an agreement with the other side, you go in front of a judge or arbitrator who decides the percentage of your responsibility in the case. If he feels you are 100% right he will say so.

He will interview you in a room with your attorney, and the other party's insurance attorney.

You are being looked at as a person and being judged for your honesty, integrity and sticking to the facts. The facts of the case are also being reviewed independently through your medical records, police reports, etc.

When you finish this process, the judge decides on a fair settlement fee. You have thirty days to accept or reject it. The other person's attorney also has thirty days to reject or accept it.

If you reject or they reject the offer, then you begin selecting a jury for a court case.

Up until the day of the court case the other person's attorney may offer you more.

Up until the day of the trial, you may change your mind and decide to take the offer.

This is costly since your lawyer has already spent hundreds or thousands of dollars preparing your case and you will owe him that out of your settlement. If you settle on the same figure earlier you avoid these costs.

CHAPTER TWO - DOCTORS

THE 1ST STEP :

The Ambulance Ride and your Hospital stay.

1. Your rights - If you choose to go to the hospital after your accident, you may choose the hospital you go to - do not let the ambulance driver choose for you. Look for a hospital with a trauma center.

2. In many cases, if there are no broken bones or obvious severe injuries, the hospital will release you as quickly as possible.

   You may still feel dizzy, in pain, disoriented, or anxious but after initial tests are taken and everything comes up negative, they will send you home. Depending on the hospital, sometimes they don't do any tests and just tell you to go see your personal physician.

3. By the way, you may be responsible for the first 20% or your deductible which usually is the ambulance ride and initial hospital stay or tests. These are the longest outstanding bills that hardly ever get paid. Even if your lawyer tells you not to pay them or not to worry about them, be careful they do not send you to collections - pay at least something toward the bill.

Finding the right doctor for you: YOUR RIGHTS

According to New Jersey Law, the first 10 days following an accident you are allowed to see and begin treatment with any doctor of any specialty that you choose - provided they are a licensed health care professional. Check with the laws in your state.

The doctor who is recommending treatment, writes a report and the medical reason or necessity for the tests or treatment he is recommending, and the insurance company has 72 hours (in NJ) to say yes or no to the treatment. Check with the laws in your state.

First Doctor to Visit: Your GP (family doctor)

Your Primary Care physician or family doctor will refer you to other specialists as needed.

Your lawyer might also give you suggestions.

Your insurance company will tell you the details of how to schedule these visits - for example, do you need a referral or authorization.

There are many rules regulating who and when you see doctors with penalties imposed if you do not follow the "care paths" outlined by the insurance companies.

Your primary care physician and even the emergency room may not always know to send you to specialists -

DO YOUR RESEARCH !!

NEUROLOGIST

Nerve problems

1. Headaches/Migraines
2. Numbness/tingling
3. Hot or Cold sensations of extremities
4. Dizziness
5. Head bruised or bleeding

ORTHOPEDIC

Spine and Bone problems

1. Fractures -Broken bones
2. Sprain/ Strain

3. Back Pain - Severe

4. Neck Pain - Severe

5. Knee pain

PAIN MANAGEMENT

ANASTHESIOLOGIST

1. Conservative treatment using medication, injections (steroid, epidurals, nerve blocks), and other minimally invasive procedures.

2. Usually the last step before surgery

NEUROSURGEON/ORTHOPEDIC SURGEON

1. Surgery specialists - Discusses the possibilities of surgery for neck and back.

CHIROPRACTOR

1. Back Pain - Mild/ Moderate

2. Neck Pain -Mild/ Moderate

PSYCHIATRIST

1. Anxiety/ Panic Attack while driving or at other times

2. Sleeplessness due to anxiety

3. Depression - Lack of drive or ambition, sadness, despair

4. Difficulty coping with the changes that the accident caused.

NEUROPSYCHOLOGIST/ PSYCHOLOGIST

1. Mild Head Injury - Memory /Concentration/ Speech Problems

2. Post Traumatic Stress - Nightmares/ flashbacks - startle easily.

3. Post Concussion Syndrome - Hit your head (front or back) with or without bleeding.

4. Anxiety/ Depression - talk therapy instead of or in addition to medication.

5. SEVERE SUICIDAL DEPRESSION CALL 911

Other Doctors that may be useful for some :

EAR NOSE AND THROAT DOCTOR -

1. Any discharge from the ear

2. Severe sinus problems not present before accident

3. Problems breathing or swallowing nor present before accident

4. Ringing in the ears

OPTHAMOLOGIST /NEURO - OPTHAMOLOGIST

Eye problems

1. Blurred vision

2. Sensitivity to light

3. Prescription change not due to age

4. Floaters or black spots

GASTROENTOROLOGIST

Stomach problems

Seatbelt trauma may include :

1. Incontinence

2. Kidney or liver dysfunction

3. Difficulty urinating

4. Stomach Pain

5. Gallbladder pain

WEAR YOUR SEATBELT - The damage is worse if you don't.

CARDIOLOGIST

Heart problems

1. Chest Pains

2. Heart Palpitations

3. Blood Pressure Changes

4. SEVERE PERSISTENT CHEST PAIN - CALL 911

There is a specialist for every condition.

If the condition was not present before the accident there is no reason to think that it is magically going to go away after the accident - get it checked out as soon as you notice it.

Some conditions that preexisted the accident may worsen after the accident. They are still covered by insurance.

Blood Pressure or Diabetes may spike due to trauma- so check it out.

Some symptoms may not be noticed until weeks after the accident.

Document any and all change in your symptoms so you can discuss them with your doctor.

The brain is only able to focus on one or two major pain areas at a time.

Sometimes a worsening (degenerative) process starts at the accident and isn't felt until later.

Check it out as soon as you feel the pain is moderate to severe.

Mild pains will either resolve quickly or get worse over time.

Only you will be able to tell initially what is painful.

Doctors are not psychics. You must tell them about your pain, even if you are not the complaining type of person.

Pain is not a sign of weakness. It is real and chances are it will not go away so quickly. Pain is a warning sign from your body that you are in trouble. Ignore it, and it will grow.

Also, tell your doctor about side effects from medication - don't just stop taking your meds because of side effects.

THINGS TO REMEMEBER FOR YOUR DOCTOR VISITS

- <u>Bring a list to your doctor of your every pain</u> . Try not to leave anything out because if you come back with a new pain in two months the doctor may become suspicious of all your pains.

- <u>Write down your questions</u> and concerns before going to the doctor.

- <u>Bring a friend</u> -you may forget what was discussed - especially if your injuries were severe and/or complicated.

- <u>Always ask for a copy of your records or reports done</u> - they belong to you but you must ask for them (there my be a fee).

Do not be afraid to complain too much about your pain . You were in a major accident!

Other specialists you may see depending on your injuries may be : <u>Urologist</u> - incontinence, bladder pain. <u>TMJ specialist</u> or <u>Oral Surgeon</u> - Jaw pain, misalignments, broken teeth, and related headaches.

HOW TO TELL A GOOD DOCTOR FROM A BAD DOCTOR :

Good Doctors :

(WEBSITE : Castleconnoly.com - This will tell you a doctor's credentials, lawsuits against them, Professional affiliations, and training. Once again, initial research will prevent later problems.)

1. Listen to you and do not minimize your complaints.

2. Make sure that tests are taken right away to determine extent of damage.

3. Offer conservative therapies first such as the following: (before talk of injections or surgery unless it is emergency surgery).

    Examples: Massage, Physical Therapy, Chiropractic, Ice and heat therapies, Ultrasound, Electric Stim Therapy, Aqua Therapy (Water therapy in a heated pool).

4. They also offer pain, anxiety, sleep, and depression medications.

5. Go over results of your tests in plain English and explain options thoroughly so that you can understand them - I.e. not in medical terms.

6. Will call and send reports to insurance companies in a timely fashion when procedures or tests that they recommend are questioned or denied by the insurance companies.

7. Coordinate your treatment with your other doctors via phone, reports, e-mail etc.

8. Are willing to testify in court or do a video deposition on your behalf should your case go to court.

9. Will not rush you out of his office each and every visit.

WHAT TO EXPECT - THE HEALING PROCESS

1. It takes time to heal from a bad accident. From months to years.

2. Many injuries are soft tissue injuries - this means the muscles, and connective tissue, ligaments, cartilage, etc. that took the brunt of the accident were traumatized and stay stuck balled up in knots for a long time - Any part of your body that is not bone is soft tissue.

    There really is no exact healing period for soft tissue injury. Everyone is different.

3. Bruises under the skin usually go away - the only bruises to worry about are the ones in the head. Any bleeding near the brain needs immediate attention and testing as well as follow up.

4. Back and neck injuries - can start as muscle and ligament problems and may deteriorate into more serious problems such as bulging and herniated discs. Discs are shock absorber gel like material between the bones of the spine. If they leak out of their fluid sac they can cause nerve damage, pain, and weakness in the muscles.

5. Shoulder injuries/ hip injuries - tears and displacements are painful and get worse without treatment.

6. Fractures/ compound breaks - These injuries have a timetable of healing - the more hardware(screws, plates, or rods) that have to be used the longer the healing time.

If you ignore these serious injuries, within months they will work into a painful situation.

Traditional care starts with :

1. Physical therapy 3 times per week for 1-3 months. If that does not work, then either more therapy or

2. Cortisone / Lidocaine injections, Nerve blocks, epidurals, or RF oblation (burning of nerves that surround pain area).

3. If that doesn't work , then surgery is discussed.

All this takes time to get approved by the insurance companies, get written up in report form by the doctor and get scheduled with the doctor's office.

Surgery can be minimally invasive or very invasive.

There are new techniques coming out all the time that are less invasive with decreased recovery time and post operative pain.

A. Minimal surgery - done in one day - no overnight stay - no big incision.

B. Invasive surgery - 1-3 nights in the hospital, long recovery period - weeks to months (up to 6 months).

Your doctor will recommend what he thinks is the best surgery for you. Keep in mind , this is based on his schooling and experience and may not be the latest techniques available.

Do your homework - look up the latest procedures and success rates. Your computer will become your best friend. If you can't go online ask family or friends for help.

Ask your doctor about some alternative surgery choices to see if you are a candidate.

Always go for a second opinion.

Surgery is a trauma to the body and the immune system.

Neck and Back Surgeries are best done by Neurosurgeons or orthopedic surgeons.

Failed neck and/or back surgeries depend on several risk factors :

1. <u>Age</u> - the older you are the harder it is for the body to recover
2. <u>Smoking</u> - Long time smokers recover slowly
3. <u>Health condition prior to surgery</u> - cardiac, diabetes, weight problems and more are all complicating risk factors in surgery
4. <u>Psychological condition prior to surgery</u>

In most cases it is a good idea to get cleared psychologically as well as physically before surgery. So have your doctor schedule you for a psychological evaluation before opening you up.

Stress plays a major role in the body's ability to recover as does certain psychological diagnoses such as severe depression, anxiety and panic, schizophrenia, and psychosis.

THERE ARE OTHER ALTERNATIVES TO SURGERY :

Early intervention is key

Consistent daily self care is essential

Find a therapy that works for you - it is a little like playing Russian roulette but it works -

Here are some options :

1. Physical therapy - heat , ice, muscle stim, ultrasound and brief massage
2. Massage - not covered by many insurances but does a world of good Hot tub, Jacuzzi, and pool therapy(also known as aqua therapy)
3. Acupuncture, Acupressure
4. Chiropractic
5. Energy therapies - Hands on Healing , Reiki, Reflexology, Shiatsu, etc.
6. Nutritional therapy - herbs, vitamins, nutrients, and homeopathy that support healing
7. Biofeedback - details the early warning signs of stress by measuring them and feeding them back to you.
8. Any combination of the above therapies

Every time you get upset, angry, or panicked - the muscles and nerves that are desperately trying to heal are tightening up and undoing all the good you've done. Guard your space - Let in only those people who are supportive and can help you heal.

Self care includes :

1. Gentle neck and back stretches

2. Support for the neck and back while sitting

3. Heat and/or ice therapy -20 minutes twice daily.

4. Gentle massage for headaches, and neck pain.

5. Topical pain rubs for temporary relief of symptoms.

Other suggestions about recovery from surgery :

Whatever the doctor says is the recovery period for your surgery - allow yourself to double it just in case.

Recovery is painful - make sure you have support to help around the house, to help you get dressed, to go shopping for you, etc.

Take it day by day - Don't lock yourself in to going back to work or school by a specific date.

Build in an exit plan for your return to school or work. See how you do, - if it is too much for you find another way - such as light duty, part time, home schooling, or even a new job. If you don't, your condition may deteriorate and need more drastic treatment.

In general, your life will change dramatically after a bad accident. Knowledge is power. Power is the ability to act and control the situation before it controls you.

Learn what you can do to help yourself

Don't overdo it

Do your research

Stress Less

Find a doctor you can trust

CHAPTER THREE - INSURANCE

The 1st step : **Call your insurance company after an accident.**

List everything that happened to the best of your recollection -

If you forget - don't be embarrassed. Try not to leave out any details of your injuries no matter how embarrassing they may be. For example, many people omit breast injuries from seatbelt trauma, or incontinence because it is embarrassing.

CHECK YOUR COVERAGE -

See what you are liable for and / or what you're entitled to.

Check to see who is the primary carrier and who is secondary.

In order to save you money, some insurance companies will have you assign your claim to your health insurance company first and your automobile company second.

IN MY OPINION IT IS NOT A GOOD IDEA TO MAKE YOUR PRIMARY COVERAGE YOUR HEALTH INSURANCE COMPANY !

1. THEY ARE NOT IN THE AUTO INSURANCE BUSINESS.

2. THEY DO NOT COVER MANY OF THE MEDICAL SERVICES THAT ARE COVERED BY AUTO INSURANCE POLICIES.

3. THE RED TAPE PAPERWORK CAN BE OVERWHELMING.

Remember, you may have coverage under your homeowners or an umbrella policy or even coverage that came with a credit card. Do your research.

VERY IMPORTANT :

1. DO NOT SIGN ANY RELEASES OR WAIVERS OF ANY KIND FOLLOWING AN ACCIDENT THAT ARE SENT TO YOU BY AN INSURANCE COMPANY.

2. DO NOT ACCEPT OR DEPOSIT ANY CHECK THAT SAYS FINAL PAYMENT UNTIL YOU SPEAK YO YOUR LAWYER.

3. DO NOT RELEASE ANY MEDICAL RECORDS TO THE OTHER PERSON'S INSURANCE COMPANY - CALL YOUR LAWYER IMMEDIATELY. NOTIFY YOUR INSURANCE COMPANY.

4. YOU HAVE 1 YEAR FROM THE DATE OF ACCIDENT IN MOST STATES TO FILE A LAW SUIT. IF YOU ARE NOT SATISFIED WITH HOW THE INSURANCE COMPANY IS DEALING WITH YOUR MEDICAL CARE - CALL A LAWYER AND START A CASE.

5. THE PERSON WHO HIT YOU WILL HAVE THEIR INSURANCE COMPANY CALL YOU TO SETTLE YOUR CLAIM - DO NOT SETTLE YOUR CLAIM UNTIL YOU SPEAK WITH YOUR LAWYER FIRST.

6. YOUR SETTLEMENT PHASE AND NEGOTIOATIONS BEGIN RIGHT AFTER THE ACCIDENT AND CONTINUE UNTIL YOUR INJURIES ARE HEALED OR BECOME PERMANENT - FROM THAT TIME ON YOU HAVE TWO YEARS TO SETTLE YOUR CASE (NJ LAW) -Check with your own state for differences.

INSURANCE COVERAGE :

There are 2 types of policies you can choose :

Basic or Standard .

The Basic is less expensive .

IT IS BEST TO CHOOSE THE STANDARD POLICY.

This is advice after the fact, since you have already had your accident and whatever coverage you have is already in play, but spread the word to others - it is essential to have really good coverage in a bad accident.

PIP COVERAGE :

Personal Injury Protection (PIP) has 2 parts :

1. Pays for medical expenses
2. Pays for other expenses - such as lost wages, travel to doctors, essential services (Cleaning the house , mowing the lawn, etc.)

PIP, may also be known as no fault insurance, which means that your insurance company immediately begins paying for your medical expenses regardless of whose at fault.

When you call your insurance company to file a claim, you make your first impression. Be truthful and to the point.

In most instances, your insurance agent or representative will be very sympathetic to your plight and try to help you navigate the maze of doctors that you may need to start treating with.

The first 10 days following an accident are crucial because you can go to see any doctor or licensed health care professional and start any treatment without prior authorization from the insurance company. After the first 10 days, every treatment or doctor's visit must be authorized first by your auto insurance company.

Some insurance carriers assign your case to a nurse case manager who oversees your medical issues. She/He may accompany you to your doctor's appointment or call you afterwards to see how you are.

The insurance company is a business with a bottom line to look at. As in all businesses, let's just say that some insurance companies are better at customer service than others.

The case managers and adjusters work for the insurance company and you, the consumer.

They are caught in the middle between bottom line dollars and you - the person who has paid premiums on time for years.

Although the case manager may be sympathetic in the beginning, there comes a time where they may feel that you have had enough treatment before you or your doctor say you are ready.

Most of the time, in the beginning of your case, the insurance company goes along with any tests your doctor feels are warranted and medically necessary.

Occasionally, they may initially deny a test saying that it is not necessary at this point.

It may be as easy as a letter from the doctor stating why this test is necessary with more specific information. A letter from your lawyer might also get things moving in your direction.

Follow up with phone calls to your insurance company. Don't forget to document date and time and who you speak to.

Assertive and not aggressive is the rule of thumb.

HINT : THE SQUEEKY WHEEL GETS THE GREASE

Be persistent without being a pest.

The insurance company will not deny you care unless they are suspicious of fraud or foul play. So, in theory, you should get the treatment you need.

If your test results are positive - meaning something is showing up on the tests, you are more likely to get the treatment that you need.

The tests can be X-ray, Magnetic Resonance Imaging (MRI), CAT scan, Electromyogram, Sonogram, Disco gram, Bone scan, or bone density test.

These tests determine the extent of bone damage, spine or disc damage, and/or nerve damage.

When the test results are negative and you are still in agonizing pain, they may send you to a pain management specialist or a psychologist for further evaluation.

Many soft tissue injuries (muscles, ligaments, etc.) do not show up on tests and are hard to prove.

Muscle tension, tight ligaments and some tears and herniations, depending on where they are and depending on the expertise of the X-ray technician may not be detected right away.

You may want to go get a second opinion - that is your right.

Other options at your disposal if you are not happy with injections, psychotherapy, or medications are physical therapy, chiropractic, or acupuncture which could be prescribed to relieve the pain.

As far as psychological evaluation goes-

It doesn't mean that the pain is in you head .

It may mean that the anxiety, sleeplessness, stress, and/ or depression are causing your symptoms to become worse. Check it out - better safe than sorry. Counseling after a major accident can make the difference between healthy recovery and a chronic trauma that may haunt you the rest of your life.

If the insurance company suspects foul play, they may have you followed and videotaped. All they need to see is you taking out the garbage, raking the leaves, or even carrying groceries into your home, to make a good case in front of a judge or jury.

That's why I say - don't push it - let your body heal. If your doctor says don't do something then don't do it.

Even though you will feel helpless, bored, or less than a man or woman - this healing time is critical.

This time is your healing window, the best chance you have to heal. Don't blow it and risk further complications down the line.

Pain that is not tended to tends to get worse.

Muscle or ligament tears develop, herniations degenerate and get worse, displacements of shoulder and hips worsen and arthritis may develops over time.

Take care of these pains early and you won't have problems later.

HOW THE SYSTEM WORKS

PIP - PERSONAL INJURY PROTECTION

Medical expenses and related expenses are reimbursed initially. Eventually , your insurance company goes after the at fault driver's insurance company to pay for your medical bills.

Other expenses related to your case involve

- Medication reimbursement
- Travel and gas expense to your doctor's appointments
- Meals and lodging to travel and see a specialist far away
- Essential services
- Lost wages, income, or school time
- Lost property

Essential services are duties that you cannot perform due to your injuries . These may include:

- doing the laundry
- mowing the lawn
- shoveling snow
- cleaning your house.

Your reimbursement for each essential service is between $12.00 to $20.00 per day. This type of protection only works when you are clearly not at fault. When you are at fault in an accident, your Bodily Injury Liability and Property Damage Liability takes over. In addition, your own insurance company will provide a lawyer for you. Coverages range from $15k - $250k.

For most insurance companies, you are responsible for 20% of all bills incurred for the first $5000.00 of treatment depending on your policy.

This usually includes ambulance ride from scene of accident and hospital stay and tests. It may also include your family doctor or the first doctor you treat with. If you can't afford it - don't ignore it - work out a payment plan.

You will get bills for this. As long as you pay at least something monthly towards those bills you will not go to collections.

Do not just forward these bills to your lawyer- you will get sent to collections for these bills and your credit will be affected.

Some policies also provide for income continuation paying you for work that you miss due to your accident - check your policy.

In a 1 vehicle accident (pedestrian, hit a tree or pole, parked car,) your insurance company pays.

IN A 2 VEHICLE ACCIDENT -

A. <u>If you are at fault</u> - your insurance company pays the other person's bills and your medical bills up to your policy limit.

B. <u>If you are not at fault</u> - the other person's insurance ultimately pays but your own insurance picks up the immediate medical expenses for immediate care injuries.

C. <u>If you are a passenger</u> injured in someone else's car or you were driving someone else's car, their insurance pays for medical bills until fault is determined.

OTHER RESOURCES YOU CAN USE -

Many states have resources as part of their health and human services programs. One such department helps you get back on your feet after your accident. It is called DVR.

DVR - The Division of Vocational Rehabilitation can help you with your employment needs. It helps with finding a new job or keeping your existing job. Funding for schooling, career testing, counseling and providing you with a job coach may also be part of your benefits if you qualify. All at no cost to you. It is a state sponsored program.

135 East State Street

PO Box 398

Trenton, New Jersey 08625-0398

(609) 292-5987 ; (609) 292-8347; (609) 292-2919 (TDD)

The TBI Fund - The Traumatic Brain Injury Fund in many states provides assistance and money for services you may need if you sustained a head injury in an accident. It is a division of Disability Services within the Department of Human Services of New Jersey. When insurance is exhausted or unavailable to meet a person with a head injury's needs the TBI Fund takes over.

TBI FUND FAMILY HELP Line is (800)669-4323

To apply for assistance call - (888)285-3036

The Department of Banking and Insurance -

Its mission is to regulate the insurance industry among other industries in the state. To protect and educate consumers as well as promote the growth of the industries they represent.

20 West State Street

PO BOX 325

Trenton , New Jersey 08625

(609) 292-7272   Hotline : 1 800 446 7467

For complaints call :

Consumer Inquiry and Case Preparation Unit -

Inquiries and Complaints

PO Box 471

Trenton , New Jersey 08625-0471

(609)633-1882

Email : ellen.derosa@dobi.state.nj.us

Insurance claims Ombudsman - consumer advocate provides info on insurance related issues

PO Box 472

Trenton, New Jersey 08625

Email : ombudsman@dobi.state.nj.us

The insurance company may use any one of the following systems to check the validity of your treatments or tests.

THE AUTHORIZATION :

By law , the insurance company has 72 hours to get back to you with an authorization for services or a denial of services.

When you send anything to the insurance company, send it return receipt requested. Make sure you keep copies of all important documents. Also fax a copy to them right away and get a person's name to confirm they got the fax you just sent and call to confirm that it arrived.

MEDICAL REVIEW :

Medical review is a process that takes more time when you need treatment.

It works like this - a nurse or a doctor - who does not necessarily specialize in the field of medicine that you have your injuries in, will determine that :

a. a) treatment is not warranted at this time or
b. b) will adjust the treatment length that your specialist doctor recommends.
c. c) treatment is experimental and therefore denied
d. d) treatment is not medically necessary at this time

This requires your doctor's office to submit an appeal - a process that can take up to a month or two further delaying your treatment.

Speak to your lawyer - legally they can't stop treatment until they have a specialist in the same field determine that you do not need treatment.

PAYMENT PROBLEMS :

Sometimes insurance companies delay payment after they have authorized treatment. Authorization is not a guarantee of payment. If your doctor's office is not getting paid, and the bill runs up over thousands of dollars, they may not continue to treat you.

Advocate for yourself and use your lawyer. If all else fails, there is a process called PIP arbitration -where an impartial judge decides if you should continue treatment and if your doctor should get paid.

Lawyers usually try to save this arbitration for the end of treatment when a whole pile of bills are not paid.

INDEPENDENT MEDICAL EXAMINATION (IME)

IME stands for Independent Medical Evaluation. In theory, it is good to get checked out by another doctor somewhere down the line to avoid fraud or just to get another opinion.

The IME doctor is paid by the insurance company and may give you a fair assessment or may be dispassionate and dismissive.

This doctor is not a second opinion for you, only for the insurance company.

He/She may be compassionate and spend time with you listening to your complaints or they may dismiss you within the first 10 minutes of your visit having already made up their minds.

He/She will not treat you or give you medical advice. Chances are they will not answer your medical questions.

A complete physical exam of the injured area should take place. It is your legal right to have an examination done. If this does not happen contact your lawyer immediately.

All MRI and test results should be forwarded to this IME doctor but sometimes important records are left out.

Bring your own copies of all your films and their interpretations.

Bring a friend (witness) with you. Some doctors are fair and honest in what they see and others are less than fair.

During the IME exam do not allow your doctor to move your body in any way that causes excruciating pain. If he continues to try, tell him to stop, If he persists, then refuse again to be moved and begin to walk out of the door. The interview is over. If the doctor made your condition worse tell your lawyer about it. Call your lawyer right there in the doctor's office. Or when you get home, write down exactly what happened as you see it. Get your lawyer to reschedule with another doctor.

The insurance company cannot legally discontinue treatment if the IME has not determined that it be discontinued.

So, if you are waiting to get an appointment for an IME do not let your insurance company discontinue treatment pending IME results - call your lawyer and get back in treatment until the IME says it is not needed anymore.

Losing treatment time may worsen your condition and you may loose weeks to months before a determination is made.

The IME must be a specialist in the same field of medicine that you are treating for. For example, a general practitioner cannot say that you do not need neurological care. Call your lawyer immediately if you suspect that this is happening. The specialty of the IME doctor should be listed in the letter you get from the insurance company telling you the time and place of the meeting.

The IME appointment must be within local traveling distance to your home unless there is no one else in that specialty that has a practice near you.

DO NOT LET THEM SEND YOU ON A LONG DISTANCE TRIP FOR AN IME IF THERE IS A DOCTOR NEAR YOU WHO CAN DO THE IME - CALL YOUR LAWYER IMMEDIATELY AND GET THE APPOINTMENT CHANGED TO A MORE LOCAL DOCTOR.

MAXIMUM MEDICAL IMPROVEMENT (MMI) :

You are still in pain, but you get a letter stating that it has been determined (by IME or insurance in-house doctor) that you have reached maximum medical benefit, this means that they feel there is nothing more that can be done for you. This is not the end. Contact your lawyer immediately and he will direct you on what to do next.

As time goes on, if you can work you will have an income. If you are not working and you are an employee, you may have short term disability which will not be enough in most cases to pay the bills.

If the case continues beyond 6 months you are looking at applying for more permanent social security/disability. This is a whole new hassle of paperwork, denials, red tape, reapplication - altogether a very tiring affair.

TYPICAL PROBLEMS

1. What to do if you get a denial for a service you need ?

    Appeal it - that's your right - talk to our lawyer and doctor.

2. What happens if you talk to a non - cooperative insurance person ?

    Immediately ask to speak to a supervisor .

3. What if I still can't get results ?

If complaints reach a peak of intolerance you can always contact the Better Business Bureau and even more importantly, the New Jersey Department of Banking and Insurance. Your lawyer should know this information.

Denial or delay of your treatment will cost your health dearly. Your health will get worse, in most cases, without consistent treatment.

Each time they delay treatment for months at a time your condition may deteriorate further - both mentally and physically.

Unless you have a NO lawsuit threshold , you will not get paid for pain and suffering. Your medical bills will get paid but the precious time and energy, loss of income, and sometimes the loss of house and home , wife and family will never be repaid.

The fight to get money you paid in good faith in premiums to the insurance carriers requires a whole troop of hard headed billing department personnel from all your doctor's offices.

PIP (personal injury protection) has 3 parts:

1. Covers your medical expenses
2. Covers related expenses such as travel to doctors, lost wages, expenses related to your case

3. Essentials services - most people don't know about this - the insurance company will pay up to $20.00/ day for you to have people come to your house to clean, do laundry , mow the lawn , etc - work you cannot do because of your injuries. Each of these expenses are reimbursed separately at $20.00 /day - Check your policy.

You are compensated for the following in a law suit case if you have a no law suit threshold:

1. Lost wages, school time, or income
2. Medical bills
3. Loss of consortium - the ability or desire to have sex with your partner
4. Pain and suffering

<u>**A Lawsuit Threshold**</u> means that you have signed off on not being able to sue the party that hit you for pain and suffering. This lowers your monthly premiums.

You may also be encouraged to lower your monthly premiums by lowering your deductibles, liability and personal injury coverage.

You may also be encouraged to lower your maximum medical expense from the standard policy of $250,000.00 to the Basic policy of $15,000. This is how some companies save you money !

This means that after your deductible, the insurance company will only pay $15,000 toward your medical expenses. Considering doctor's and hospital fees today, not to mention if you should need surgery ($10,000-$20,000 average fees), you will run out of money in no time.

It saves you money in the short term, but will keep you from getting the treatment and money you need in the event of a catastrophe.

<u>**No Lawsuit Threshold**</u> means that no matter what happens you can sue for pain and suffering over and above your medical expenses.

Look folks, you are gambling with your life and your health. I don't mean to scare you, but once you are in a bad accident and you don't have the right coverage, you are in trouble.

Get the best policy money can buy, cover yourself with a warm blanket of maximum coverage and don't give up your right to sue.

I know that all this information has been one sided in favor of you the patient. There are some good agents, case workers, doctors, and lawyers out there who are truly looking out for your welfare. And, thank God for them.

This book was written to speak to those of you who are finding it difficult, if not impossible, to get the care you need because one of the professionals on your team is not doing their job.

Knowing your rights, and knowing how to make people accountable for their wrongdoings will get you back on track and back to your life.